ROSSI'S

THE STORY OF SOUTHEND'S
FAVOURITE ICE CREAM

BY PATRICIA VOLANTE

Best wishes
Patricia Volante.

 ESTUARYPUBLISHING

First published 2018

Estuary Publishing

www.estuarypublishing.co.uk

A CIP catalogue record for this book is available from the British Library.

ISBN 978-1-9999935-0-4

Printed and bound in Great Britain by Clays Ltd, Elcograf S.p.A.

Contents

For Enzo and Riccardo

In Memory of Fernando

About The Author

It's funny how an argument with your Dad over pocket money can change your whole life! I was just fifteen and wanted more money to buy records and hang out with my friends in the Sorrento coffee bar in Southend High Street, or drink Russian tea in the Shrubbery Cafe on Royal Terrace. In those days most people left school and started work at fifteen, but I was staying on at school. So, on Easter Saturday 1959, I found myself in Southend High Street looking for a Saturday job. I tried Marks and Spencer and Woolworths, but there were no vacancies - or perhaps the sight of me with my pudding basin haircut and ankle socks didn't inspire much confidence in my ability to cope behind a busy counter.

As I left Woolworths I glanced into Rossi's Temperance Bar which was next door. A sign in the window said: "Vacancies". I can vividly remember walking into the busy shop. Along the left-hand side, customers sat around wooden tables on bench seats covered in red leather. There had once been cubicles there, but by 1959 they had been removed and the interior of the shop had been modernised and new glass doors added. On the right-hand side of the shop, people were seated on high stools at the bar with its stainless-steel fascia. Behind the counter there was an array of shiny chrome water heaters, coffee machines, glass cabinets full of sandwiches and cakes and a large ornate till. Four members of staff in crisp white overalls were busy serving customers. I remember the noise of the steam as the milk was heated, the clink of cups, and the 'kerching' of the till, the general din of people chatting as they ate and the smell of fresh coffee. Ice cream was being sold from a counter at the front of the shop, and as I stood waiting for someone to notice me, I heard a bell ring and a voice call out "Cheese on toast!" from the kitchen. As the cook peered through the serving hatch and handed a plate to one of the staff, I managed to catch her eye and she asked me if I was being served. I explained that I was looking for a Saturday job and waited while she summoned the manageress, who asked if I could start straight away. Before I knew what had hit me, I was behind the counter in a spotless white overall, embroidered with "Rossi" in red on the lapel. It came down to my ankles and was so starched that it could have stood up by itself. From that day on, I worked at Rossi's most Saturdays, Sundays and during the school holidays. Even when I went to college, there was always a holiday job there for me.

A corner of Rossi's 37-39 High St in the 1950s

I did a lot of my studies at the ice cream counter, perched on a stool reading English and French literature for my A' levels between serving customers and eating the chocolate flakes meant for the 'Rossi 99' ice creams. Fernando Rossi, who spoke fluent French, was always on hand to help and we shared so many interests. I left school with no idea what I wanted to do, but with a top A' level grade in Art I embarked on a five-year foundation course at art school. I was so bored after two years that I left and went to stay with a friend in Paris for a few months, helping in her parents' café.

Fernando had always described himself as a 'confirmed bachelor' despite several attractive young ladies who came into the shop to see him. So, when he wrote to me in Paris and said that he missed having me around I was delighted. We started going out together when I got back and when four years and three jobs later I decided to go to university and study for a B.Ed. majoring in French he was there to help and encourage me again.

The Author in 1974

I graduated in July 1971 and two months later Fernando and I were married. After the birth of our three children, Carlo, Annalisa and Isabella, I started writing down interesting facts that Fernando told me about the business and the family in one of the children's baby books. Sadly, Fernando died in 1987. But my life was to take an unexpected but very happy turn, as ten years later I married Riccardo Volante, another member of the Rossi family.

I had spent many hours talking and looking at old photographs with Fernando's mother Anna Rossi before she died in 1975, and of course over the years I have spent a lot of time in Valvori and Vallerotonda, the Italian villages where Anna and Agostino Rossi had lived before coming to Britain. It isn't difficult to imagine the sadness that they must have felt, nor the courage it took, to leave such beautiful places behind.

This is their story and the story of Southend-on-Sea's famous Rossi Ice Cream. I would like to dedicate it to my grandson Enzo who inspired me to write it and my husband Riccardo who spurred me on.

Author Patricia and her husband Riccardo

Acknowledgements

I would like to thank:

Estuary Publishing, especially my publisher Audrey Snee, for her patience, as the few pages I had originally written for Enzo grew into a book and for guiding me through the whole publishing process.

Karen Wells, Chris Price, Roberto and Dino Rossi for sharing their memories. Carlo, Annalisa and Isabella Rossi for their enthusiasm and suggestions.

To all those who allowed me to use family portraits in this book.

Tim Severwright and Ray Newman my 'Beta' readers for their interest and suggestions.

Colin Gray, Director of Rossi's Southend-on-Sea Ltd for showing me how far the manufacture of Rossi's ice cream has advanced, since Agostino Rossi began one hundred years ago.

Chapter 1

From Vallerotonda to Glasgow

Agostino c.1917

Massimiliano Agostino Antonio Rossi, known as Agostino or Gus to family and friends, was born on the 24th January 1889, in Vallerotonda, a small Italian village, on the edge of the Abbruzzo National Park in the Lazio region, about 100 kilometres from Rome and a short drive from the famous Abbey of Monte Cassino. Agostino lived with his parents, Giuseppe and Vincenza Rossi, his brother Silvino and sisters Elenuccia and Erminia.

When Agostino was a young boy there were few occupations apart from working on the land. Most families supported themselves by growing olives, grapes, citrus fruits, tomatoes and vegetables. Others grew 'gran turco' a kind of maize, which they sold to other villagers who would have it ground to make flour for bread, pasta or polenta. Families also kept chickens, goats and pigs. The pigs would feed on acorns and truffles in the autumn and they were then slaughtered and made into prosciutto, salami and delicious sausages stuffed with orange peel, spices and pork. The sausages were dried and conserved in oil. Thrushes were a delicacy when they had been feeding on the olives and were roasted and eaten whole. Tomatoes, artichokes and peppers were bottled for the winter months and families would exchange their produce for other foods they needed, like buffalo milk to make mozzarella. Goat's milk was made into ricotta or large pecorino cheeses which could also be bartered or sold. Agostino's relatives were more fortunate than many in the village. They had their own pieces of land, where they grew grapes, olives and other produce. Their olives were added to those of other olive growers in the village and made into olive oil and they made their own wine. Then as now, Italians had the ability to make delicious meals from the few ingredients they had, but they needed money as well. There was grinding poverty in the villages and small towns. There just wasn't enough work to go around, so millions of Italians were forced to leave their homes; some moved to the industrial north of Italy while others emigrated.

Many people from Agostino's village emigrated to France, but Agostino's uncle, Carmine Rossi, had already left Vallerotonda and was working in a lemonade factory in Glasgow, Scotland. So, in 1901, when he was 12 years old, Agostino travelled to Glasgow, where he joined his uncle making up flavoured syrups that were used in the making of bottles of pop. There are many stories about poor and often illiterate Italians being encouraged to pay for a ship passage to New York, only to find that the ship was going no further than Glasgow when they reached the UK. Others were led to believe that they had arrived in New York and when they found out differently, they had no choice but to stay and try to make a living. Carmine had set out from Italy intending to travel to America where he had other relatives. It isn't clear why he ended up in Glasgow instead, but neither he nor Agostino had intended to stay in Britain, and initially they tried to save enough money to buy a ticket to travel on to America. Two years later however, Carmine decided to put his savings into a small ice cream business.

In the early 1900s there were no ice cream vans so Agostino, now fourteen years old, pushed a barrow around the streets selling his uncle's ice cream. He would imitate the other Italian ice cream sellers who walked through the streets and parks ringing a bell and calling out "Hokey Pokey!" Fernando once told me that the phrase "Hokey Pokey" was first popularised in Britain in the 19th century by Italians. It was a corruption of their street cry in Italian dialect, "Ha 'n poco di gelato!" meaning 'I've got some ice cream'. It became shortened to "Ho 'n poco" and sounded like "Hokey Pokey" to their customers, who would call them the 'Hokey Pokey' men.

Things became very difficult at times when rival ice cream makers chased Agostino and deliberately spoiled his container of ice cream by putting horse manure in it. There was so much competition between the ice cream vendors that Agostino would sometimes put silver 3d pieces into his uncle's ice cream to get people to buy his rather than someone else's. He would sell an ice cream cone for one half penny, but the customers knew that it might have a small silver three penny piece in it. It usually worked and the idea that if you gave something away one day, the customers would come back the next sowed the seeds for his own business later on. Agostino had had very little schooling before leaving Italy, so he set about learning to read and write in both English and Italian, getting up at six in the morning to go to his lessons before starting work.

Fed up with pushing an ice cream barrow around for his uncle, Agostino decided to go into business with a friend who came from a neighbouring village in Italy. His friend's name was Giuseppe 'Peppino' Vettese and he had bought a bus. Peppino drove the bus, and Agostino collected the fares. At the time, there were only private bus companies in Scotland, so anyone could own a bus and drive it wherever they liked. Sometimes there were arguments and even fights between the owners of buses over who owned which routes. Agostino and Peppino were sometimes threatened by other drivers, who would come after them brandishing a heavy starting handle and shouting abuse, because they had strayed onto a route already claimed by another driver. Unfortunately, Agostino presented an easy target because he was rather short. So Peppino sold the bus and they went their separate ways. Agostino decided to try his hand at making his own ice cream and rented a small shop with some money he had saved.

While researching the family tree I found Agostino in the Scottish 1911 Census. It shows that at the age of 22 years he was living in Wardrop Street in Paisley, a suburb of Glasgow, and he had already set up his own ice cream business at 4 Lawn Street, in an area known as Paisley Cross. He is listed as an employer and the entry shows that he had been joined by his brother Silvino who was employed as a shop assistant. There were no government hand-outs for immigrants in those days, but it was common practice for people like Agostino, who had managed to establish themselves, to help family or friends emigrate by offering them work. The entry in the 1911 census shows that he was also employing three friends from his village in Italy to sell his ice cream. They are recorded as being ice cream dealers on the census, but in time they too went on to establish their own ice cream businesses. Their names are easily recognisable, as many of their relatives still live in the villages of

Anna Rossi (kneeling) and cousins washing clothes in the river c.1915

Valvori and Vallerotonda today. The Scottish Valuation Rolls show that by 1915, Agostino was renting premises at 2 Lawn Street, in addition to 4 Lawn Street, and by 1920 he was also renting a garage.

Agostino returned to his family in Italy as often as he could and on one of these trips, in 1917, he saw an attractive young lady from the next village with a group of women doing their washing down at the river. There was no running water in the houses. Some people had wells, but usually groups of women would go to do their washing in the river, rubbing their garments on the rocks with homemade soap made from olive oil.

Women were chaperoned everywhere they went. If a boy wanted to go out with a girl, he could only do so under the watchful eye of a parent or relative who would accompany them on walks and usually insisted on walking between them. So, when Agostino saw Anna, he couldn't approach her, but he discreetly made inquiries to find out who she was.

Anna lived in the neighbouring village, Valvori, about three kilometres from Vallerotonda. Anna's parents were Francesco, whose surname was also Rossi, and Eleanora Volante. The family were well respected in the village because Anna's uncle, Don Benedetto Rossi, was the first parish priest to live there. Before Don Benedetto became a priest, Mass had to be said by a priest who would visit once a month. Sometimes these priests had to travel from as far afield as Naples. At the time, girls weren't sent to school, but were expected to learn to cook and sew at home.

There wasn't a school in the village so Don Benedetto and Anna's father, Francesco, ran a school in a room in their house and taught the local children to read and write. The little 'viale' in which Don Benedetto and the family lived was later named Via Don Benedetto Rossi in memory of him.

Anna's father Francesco Rossi in Valvori, 26th June 1871

As families from Italy found work abroad and built up successful businesses, money was sent back to their villages to help support their families and in Valvori money was also donated to renovate and furnish the beautiful church of Santa Maria Addolorata, which stands in the village piazza. It was the practice in the 19th century to add another room to the house when a son in the family married. The new wife usually lived with the husband's family and as the family grew, their home grew too. Anna's home was, and still is, a large rambling place. As letters started to arrive for families in the village from abroad, Francesco and Anna's brother Amadeo decided to turn a room at the front of the house into a post office and Amadeo became the postmaster. The room is still referred to as 'La Posta' today. It's the room I like sleeping in best when I visit. Many years later a new post office was built in the village, which was run by Bruna, Amadeo's daughter. Bruna still lives in the house with all its memories. It's a sunny place where a warm welcome awaits the family whenever they feel like reconnecting with their roots and enjoying the food, scenery and fresh mountain air.

Anna once told me that when Agostino decided to ask her parents if he could write to her from Scotland, she liked him so much that she did something which was considered to be really 'forward' in those days; she sent him a photograph of herself! In 1918, they married in Valvori and Agostino took his bride back to Glasgow, to his small shop and the tenement in Wardrop Street, Paisley. Six of their seven children Bice, Vitalina (Lina), Manfredo (Fred), Fernando, Ugo and Alda were born there.

Anna and Agostino in 1925

It must have been grim for Anna at first. She was used to living with her family in a large airy house, with beautiful scenery, sunshine, fresh mountain air and warm dry winters. Now she was living in three rooms in a dingy tenement in Glasgow, where compared to Italy, it was always cold and very often wet even in the summer months. She knew no one, she couldn't speak English and she was very lonely, but like Agostino, she would eventually learn to speak English with a Scottish accent that she never lost. Life may have been difficult, but Agostino was hard working and resourceful; determined to make a success of his business and to improve his family's quality of life.

Anna Rossi in 1920 with their first child Bice. Note her melancholy expression.

Bice and Lina Rossi in Paisley c.1925

By 1925, Agostino had both a house and a shop in Paisley High Street - an indication that his Rossi ice cream had really taken off and life was getting easier. He had left the overcrowded and dismal tenement in Wardrop Street behind. Agostino was selling ice creams for a penny or a halfpenny as well as coffees, teas, chocolate, cigarettes and other confectionery. He was always experimenting and trying to improve his product. He used to say that if the ice cream was made using only the best ingredients, more of it could be eaten than other brands which had higher sugar and fat content and were full of air. He and his brother Silvino had concocted a raspberry flavoured sauce to pour onto the vanilla ice cream, which was very popular. No one else knew how to make it, and it was probably based on the flavourings Agostino had helped to make in the lemonade factory. By 1928, Silvino had his own ice cream parlour in Well Street, Paisley.

In the 1920s, Glasgow was teeming with Italian cafés, many selling ice cream in the summer and fish and chips in the winter. At first, Agostino could make enough money in the summer months to see him through the winter, but as both competition and his family grew, he decided to seek new opportunities by heading south. In 1930 the family moved from Paisley to Stockton-on-Tees, a mining community near Durham, where another family member already had a café at 81 Stockton High Street. Perhaps Agostino was thinking of starting a new venture there, but while in Stockton, Agostino's two-year-old son Massimo died of meningitis. Naturally, Anna was distraught. She wanted to go back to Italy. She hated the cold, wet, weather so Agostino decided to move to the south of England, in the hope that the weather would be warmer, and Anna would feel happier.

Rossi family group c.1925. L to R back row: Silvino and Agostino. Middle row: Three sisters Adelia (wife of Silvino), Anna and Aldina. Front row: Bice, Manfredo, Ugo (baby), Fernando and Lina.

Chapter 2

Coming to Southend-on-Sea

While on a trip to London, Agostino saw posters at a station, advertising 'Sunny Southend-on-Sea' and decided to have a look at the town. He arrived in Southend on a hot August bank holiday weekend in 1930. The High Street and the seafront were packed. He had never seen so many people. This was the place for him.

There was a small vacant shop called 'Newgood's Drapers' at number 37 High Street, next to Woolworths. Agostino made arrangements to take over the lease. There was enough room at the back of the shop for what became known as the 'milk house' where he would be able to install all the equipment he needed to manufacture his ice cream and another large store room. There was a basement where he would eventually install freezers. The shop itself was large enough to accommodate cubicles separated by glass panels, each one with a table and seating for six people. Best of all, crowds of people streamed past all day. It was the ideal spot.

Soon a deal was struck with Mr. Eccles who owned 'Eccles Creamery Ltd' based in Park Street and Queens Road to supply milk. Next, he found a place for the family to live at 60 Whitegate Road, just off the High Street, where they lived for several years before moving to Prittlewell Square. Eventually Agostino would also acquire the commercial lease to 39 High Street. He then merged the two premises to make one larger shop with a separate entrance to the factory reached via Clarence Street behind Millett's Outfitters store, which was on the corner.

*Bice Rossi, aged 13, working at 37 High St. She had to stand on a lemonade
box to reach the till. With some of the staff in 1933*

A newspaper advert promoting free ice creams on the day of the opening, led to queues all day outside the shop. Soon there were queues every day for 1d (one old penny) and 2d cornets and wafers. By July 1932, Agostino had acquired other premises at 1 Marine Parade and business was booming. So much so that it landed Agostino in a spot of bother. He was summoned before the courts because customers had been seen leaving his shop eating ice cream after 9.30 pm. This was in contravention of the 1928 Shops Act. Despite having staff posted at the doors and notices in the shop explaining that no ice cream could be taken into the street after hours, Agostino was fined £2 for each of five summonses.

ICE-CREAM AFTER HOURS

At Southend on Tuesday, Massimiliano Antonio Rossi, Marine Parade, Southend, was summoned for keeping open a shop in High Street for the sale of ice cream for consumption off the premises after general closing hours. There were five summonses.

Mr. R. Shorter, of the Town Clerk's Department, said that, under the Shops Act, 1928, no person was entitled to sell ice cream for consumption off the premises after 9.30 p.m. and after 10 p.m. on the " late day," which, in the case of Southend, was Saturday. On Saturday, June 25th, P.c. Theobald saw a number of people leaving defendant's premises carrying or eating ice cream between 10.5 and 10.35 p.m. The same thing happened on subsequent dates. Defendant had been warned by the police.

P.c. Theobald said defendant told him he had put up a notice that ice cream could only be sold for consumption on the premises after certain hours. The notice was on the wall in quite a conspicuous position.

P.c. Poole said he saw a doorkeeper part of the time, who intercepted people as they were leaving the premises.

P.c. Bennett said he kept observation on the shop for five to ten minutes on a Sunday night, and saw people leaving with cornets.

Defendant said during the hot weather ice cream was the main feature of the business. He was paying a large rent, £360 a year. At the time he received visits from the police he had the notices in the shop. He had put a girl at the door to tell people that ice cream purchased after hours must not be taken outside. The assistants behind the counters were also told to tell customers that ice cream was to be consumed inside the shop. He had done his best to prevent people consuming the ice cream off the premises.

Miss Bessie Archer said she had been told to stand at the door after general closing hours and tell customers not to take ice cream outside.

Miss Phyllis Fiori, manageress of the shop, said notices were put up, and girls were posted at the door.

The Chairman said the Bench had no alternative but to convict. There would be a fine of £2 on each of the five summonses.

Mr. S. Lincoln, for the defendant, gave notice of appeal.

Chelmsford Chronicle 15th July 1932

ICE CREAM AFTER HOURS

"At Southend on Tuesday, Massimiliano Antonio Rossi, Marine Parade Southend was summoned for keeping open a shop in High Street for the sale of ice cream for the consumption off the premises after general closing hours. There were five summonses.

Mr R Shorter of the Town Clerks Department, said that, under the Shop's Act 1928, no person was entitled to sell ice cream for consumption off the premises after 9.30 p.m. and after 10 p.m. on the "late day", which, in the case of Southend was Saturday. On Saturday June 25th, P.C. Theobald saw a number of people leaving defendant's premises, carrying or eating ice cream between 10.5 and 10.35 p.m. The same thing happened on subsequent dates. Defendant had been warned by the police.

P.C Theobald said Defendant told him he had put up a notice that ice cream could only be sold for consumption on the premises after certain hours. The notice was on the wall in quite a conspicuous position.

P.C. Poole said he saw a door keeper part of the time who intercepted people as they were leaving the premises.

P.c. Bennet said he kept observation on the shop for five to ten minutes on Sunday night and saw people leaving with cornets.

Defendant said during hot weather ice cream was the main feature of the business. He was paying a large rent £360 per year. At the time he received visits from the police he had the notices in the shop. He had put a girl at the door to tell customers that ice cream was to be consumed inside the shop. He had done his best to prevent people consuming the ice cream off the premises.

Miss Bessie Archer said that she had been told to stand at the door after general closing hours and tell customers not to take the ice cream outside.

Miss Phyllis Fiori, manageress of the shop, said notices were put up and girls were posted at the door.

The Chairman said the Bench had no alternative but to convict. There would be a fine of £2 on each of the five summonses.

Mr S Lincoln for the Defendant gave notice of appeal."

He wasn't alone in incurring these kinds of fines. Insert the words 'ice cream' into the National Newspaper Archives online, and you will find that in the 1930s, local newspapers up and down the country were peppered with such cases. It seems that the consumption of ice cream was considered to be somewhat decadent.

Aldina with the Rossi children, taken at Margaret Clarke's studio in Southend 1932

Anna's sister, Aldina and her brother Aurelio came to England in the 1930s and lived with Anna and Agostino. Anna was in the shop all day, so Aldina cared for the children. Aldina loved Southend and lived with the family until her death in 1972. For many years Aurelio helped make the ice cream. He got so fed up with people not being able to pronounce his name that he started telling everyone that his name was 'Charlie' and it stuck. Even the family called him 'Uncle Charlie'.

I discovered in the Southend archive library a copy of the 1933 Kelly's Directory (a trade directory that listed all businesses and tradespeople for each town in England) that Agostino and Anna had by then opened three shops in the town. They were at 1 Marine Parade, 12-14 Westcliff Esplanade, and 37 High Street. In the 1937 Kelly's Directory, Agostino is listed as also having refreshment rooms at another venue, 5 Grosvenor Place, with the ice cream being sold by Sandy Alaia. There were several other ice cream manufacturers in the town in 1937, including the Tomassi family who had a shop under the arches in Westcliff, the Di Mambro family in London Road, Westcliff and Benny Mazzone in Milton Road, Southend and of course there were the bigger companies like Walls and Eldorado. But it seems that Agostino's Rossi ice cream was very popular, because when later in 1937 another shop became vacant at 99 High Street, he was keen to buy the lease and expand his business. He asked various members of his family to help him raise some of the capital, but they weren't in a position to help. Anna had a cousin, Pietro Rossi who had also come to England from Valvori, and had an ice cream business in Consett, Durham. He and his family often visited Anna and Agostino in Southend and had seen that their business was thriving. The shop at 37 High Street stayed open from 9 a.m. until after 10 p.m. and was always busy. Very shrewdly Pietro offered to lend Agostino the money he needed, but only on condition that Agostino went into partnership with him.

Pietro Rossi with daughters Gemma, Maria Rossi (back row), Iolanda, his wife Lousia (seated centre) and son Antonio c.1938

The partnership was drawn up in 1938 and Agostino bought the property at 99 High Street which was on the corner of Cliff Town Road. The two families worked together at first, but for various reasons the partnership didn't work very well so it was dissolved as soon as Agostino had repaid the loan from Pietro in 1946. At this time, an agreement was reached between Agostino and Pietro that Agostino and his family would continue to trade in the shops at 37-39 High Street known as Rossi's Temperance Bar and at 99 High Street, known as the Milk Bar. Pietro Rossi would take over the shops at 1 Marine Parade and at Western Esplanade with his wife Luisa, son Antonio (Tony), and daughters Gemma, Maria and Iolanda. For the time being, Agostino would continue to supply the ice cream. Pietro later entered into another partnership with other relatives, the Figliolino family, who had an ice cream firm in Weymouth. The words 'Rossi of Southend, Westcliff and Weymouth' can be seen painted on the side of the building at 1 Marine Parade in some photographs and postcards.

Another view of Rossi's Milk Bar taken from Clifftown Rd c.1950

Gianni Volante (L) with his wife Bice Rossi (centre) with Ligo Rossi, outside Rossi's Milk Bar in 1948

Chapter 3

A Brush with Fascism

Agostino's children attended the Sacred Heart School in Southend from 1931 until they were thirteen years old, at which point they left school, as many children did in those days. Bice, Lina and Alda started to work in the shops, but Agostino sent Fred, Fernando and Ugo to the 'Collegio di Conti- Gentili' in Altari, Italy to further their education. Pietro's son Tony was sent there too. The Collegio di Conti- Gentili is in Alatri, a small hill town in the province of Frosinone, not far from Rome. When the boys were there between 1935 and 1939, it was a prestigious, private school which offered an education in the classics.

ALATRI - Collegio Conti-Gentili e Chiesa delle Scuole Pie

Collegio Conti-Gentili

The school was part of a seminary called Collegio delle Scuole Pie, housed in the Palazzo Conti-Gentili. It was very strict, and the boys weren't very happy there. They had been brought up to speak English, but now had to do all their studies in Italian. Their parents would send parcels and money to them and when family from Valvori and Vallerotonda visited, they would bring cakes and sweets for the boys. But these goodies were always confiscated and rarely seen again. Desperate times called for desperate measures and Ugo used to tell the family how he had once managed to attract the attention of a local boy by calling through a window. He lowered a note with coins wrapped in it down to the boy and asked him to go to the piazza and buy some sweets. Ugo spent all afternoon by the window waiting for the boy to return, but he never set eyes on him again.

Fred, Fernando and Ugo had to spend their holidays at the college, or travel to Valvori to stay with relatives. They were too young to travel back to England unaccompanied for the summer break, and in any case, the shops were far too busy for anyone to take time off to go and fetch them. In those days the road up to Valvori wasn't suitable for cars, so the boys would take a train to Cassino, the nearest town. Then they had to walk from Cassino to St Elia, a small village in the valley below Valvori, where an aunt would meet them by the fountain in the piazza, with a mule to carry their suitcases. From there they had to start the long climb up a track which wound its way through the terraces of olive groves. Today, it takes at least a quarter of an hour to negotiate all the hairpin bends going up by car. It must have taken hours to do it on foot and in the hot sun.

R to L Fred, Fernando and Ugo with their cousin Bruna
and Agostino off to college

In the years that Agostino's sons were at the Collegio Conti-Gentili, Benito Mussolini, the fascist dictator, was taking a keen interest in the state education system and in youth movements both in Italy and abroad. In 1922, he had promoted Giovanni Gentile, an Italian philosopher, educator and fascist politician, to Minister of Public Education. Gentile reformed secondary education in Italy with the goal of forming the future upper classes. The only means of accessing any kind of higher education was by gaining a place at a Liceo Classico like the one at Collegio di Conti-Gentili.

I have often wondered what possessed Agostino to send his sons to study in Italy, when the country had already become a fascist dictatorship by 1925. Today fascism is usually used as pejorative term, but to Italians like Agostino's family it might have seemed the lesser of two evils at the time. Italy was in serious disarray economically and to some degree Benito Mussolini managed to quell many of the riots and strikes that were plaguing the country. He nationalised industry bringing it under state control and attempted to build up Italy's aircraft, shipping and power industries, but with little success. Many Italians feared communism, and some looked to fascism as an answer to serious unemployment and inflation. Most hated Mussolini, but any sign of rebellion against him meant a beating or worse from Mussolini's black shirt thugs, so most people, Agostino and Anna's families among them, kept their heads down and went about their business.

For Agostino the only means of communicating with his sons was by letter while they were in Alatri and the contents of the boy's letters were vetted. The boys were made to join the 'Figlio Della Lupa' organisation, which means son of the she-wolf. The name refers to the roman myth of 'Romulo and Remo' the twin sons of Rhea a mortal princess and Mars the god of war. When Rhea discovered that some of the Roman gods were plotting to kill her sons, she put them in a basket and floated them in the River Tiber. They were found by a she-wolf who raised them as if they were her own cubs. Being a member of the 'Figlio Della Lupa' organisation was like being a cub-scout, but it was in actual fact part of the fascist movement, which one refused to join at one's peril. On one occasion, Mussolini actually visited the college, and all the students were assembled in the grounds to listen to his speech. Fernando was watching quietly, when he heard his name being called out. Someone gave him a push and he was so startled that he rushed forward, tripped up the steps and fell on his face at Mussolini's feet. Mussolini presented him with a medal for being an outstanding student.

Their sons were being taught that Mussolini was the only man who could lead Italy back to greatness and were being taught to call him 'Il Duce', but despite this, Agostino and Anna must have been very proud when Fernando was awarded a scholarship to enter the University of Rome. He was looking forward to continuing his studies but when war broke out in 1939, Anna insisted that the boys return to England immediately. Even then I doubt whether Agostino could have envisaged that Mussolini would drag Italy into a war.

Chapter 4

The War Years

Internment

Mussolini was keen to capture the support of Italians living abroad and gave direct financial aid to support the establishment of local fascist clubs in Europe, including some in towns in Britain. Membership was voluntary but by joining, Italian immigrants could access diplomatic and consular protection, as well as free social and cultural activities. As far as most Italians were concerned, they were just social clubs. I doubt whether they were any different to the club for families of Italian origin, run by the Italian Consulate, which Fernando and I took our children to in the 1970s. The children attended a free 'Italian School' on Saturdays to learn Italian. There was a Christmas party at our local club, and a wonderful 'scampagnata' (picnic) was arranged every year, where Italians from all over the region would come together and eat traditional Italian dishes, cooked al fresco.

I think it is human nature to feel suspicious of, or threatened, by situations that are foreign to us that we don't understand. Even before the Second World War, Italians in Britain were being linked to Mussolini's fascist movement by the media, intensifying their image as an "alien, outside people" and making assumptions about their loyalties. Attending fascist run clubs probably didn't help this image. At the outbreak of the war the *Daily Mail* newspaper which had supported Oswald Moseley and the British Union of Fascists in the 1930s, now led a campaign to have all aliens in Britain interned, including Italians and it set about whipping up anti-alien hysteria. Other newspapers quickly followed suit and initially, all Austrians and Germans over the age of sixteen living in Britain were interned.

On 10th June 1940, Italy entered the war. There was already general animosity and suspicion towards Italians in the country, which had been stoked by the press for weeks beforehand. The next day, Winston Churchill declared that all Italians should be rounded up. His exact words were "Collar the lot". The catch-all nature of the law meant few Italian families were untouched. Suddenly people with strong roots in Britain, who had been at the heart of their community, found themselves wrenched away from their families and behind barbed wire in internment camps all over Britain. This happened regardless of the fact that many had lived in the country for decades and some had even fought with the Allies in the First World War. Most Italians were interned in camps on the Isle of Man, where they had to go before a tribunal which was supposed to decide how serious a risk the internees were to national security. It was a threatening place. The camps were run by the Italians themselves, most of whom had no interest in politics whatsoever. Now they found themselves bullied and intimidated by a small number of fascist thugs in the camps.

Internees were classified into groups. Group A were people who had been in Britain for less than twenty years and those who were considered to be a high security risk or a potential threat if Britain were to be invaded. They were often deported to Canada and Australia. Group B comprised of those who were doubtful cases. After a year or two they were allowed to leave the internment camps but had to report all their movements to their local police force. The majority of Italians were in Group C, and once processed, they were free to leave with certain restrictions on their movements. Women weren't interned but restrictions were placed on their travel, and no Italian men in any category were allowed to live in coastal areas. Many internees volunteered for the Pioneer Corps as labourers for the British Army because it was a means of getting an early release from the camps.

Agostino and Anna were lucky and were not interned. They were placed in Category C and were told by the authorities that they were free, so long as they remained 30 miles away from the coast. Fortunately, Agostino and Anna had relatives who had an ice cream parlour in Lampton Road, Hounslow so they stayed with them until their restrictions were lifted in 1943.

For some inexplicable reason, Anna's brother Aurelio fell into category A and he was somewhat surprised to find himself under suspicion of being a Fifth Columnist even though he had no idea what it meant. Like the vast majority of Italians in Britain, he certainly didn't support Mussolini or Hitler. Not that that made any difference when two very apologetic, local policemen arrived at his front door to arrest him and he was bundled off to the Onchen Camp on the Isle of Man. It was just one of the many anomalies and injustices that befell hundreds of perfectly innocent men; however, Aurelio considered himself very lucky not to have been deported like many men in this category. He was luckier still, not to have been among those internees who tragically lost their lives when the Arandora Star was torpedoed.

The Arandora Star set out from Liverpool, on her way to

internment camps in Canada, with more than 1,600 passengers and crew. There were 734 Italian internees, 479 German internees – mostly Jewish refugees, 86 German prisoners of war, 200 military guards and her crew of 174 officers and men on board. She was sunk by a single torpedo from a German U-boat on 2nd July 1940 off the coast of Ireland. Two days later, the *Glasgow Herald* newspaper published an interview with one of the survivors. Otto, a German Jewish refugee, was being deported aboard the Arandora Star when it was sunk. According to Otto, the escape of many internees was made impossible because of the way they were penned in by "barbed wire strung along the deck, railings and upper structures." Among the 860 survivors were 264 Italians and 322 Germans. They were picked up by the crew of a Canadian destroyer who took them back to a Scottish port.

I was interested to note that on the records for those interned on the Isle of Man, Aurelio wrote only that he was from the province of Frosinone and perhaps intentionally, avoided mentioning Valvori. This was possibly because he feared that his presence in Britain might have serious implications for the family left in Valvori if the Germans had ever found out about it. In fact, Anna's cousin Clarissa's house was blown up by the Germans because of their connection to England and Clarissa and her husband were lucky not to have been in Vallerotonda, but in England at the time.

Apart from internment, Italy's entry into the war had another devastating effect on many Italians in Britain who, for the most part, worked hard and like Agostino and Anna had family members who were contributing to the British war effort, in spite of having relatives living in Italy. Across the country on 10th and 11th of June 1940, there were attacks on Italian businesses; including at least one incident in Southend High Street, when bricks were thrown through the windows of a delicatessen owned by an Italian family called Offredi. Italians were 'roughed up' verbally if not physically.

It was particularly hurtful when this kind of abuse came from customers they had often served in their shops. Thankfully the Rossi shops were spared any kind of unpleasantness and between 1940 and 1943 Agostino's children kept the business running under the watchful eye of family friends.

Chapter 5

The Rossi War Effort

Fred home on leave with sisters Alda (left)
and Bice at Prittlewell Square 1940

Fred was the first of Agostino's sons to go into the British Army. He had a dreadful time driving ammunition trucks in North Africa; in constant danger of being strafed by German aircraft and blown to pieces. Fred rarely spoke about it, except later in life, when he would comment on how daft he and his young comrades had been because their first instincts had been to dive under the ammunition trucks when they saw the approaching aircraft.

Fernando (left) in the Royal Hampshire Regiment

A year after Fred went into the army, Fernando joined the Infantry of the Royal Hampshire Regiment. He was stationed in Hyères, in the south of France, and then in Holland. As well as English, Fernando spoke fluent Italian, French and German, and Anna once told me that while in France he had volunteered to take part in an important "mission". His commanding officer had telephoned Anna and Agostino to ask their permission, as the mission involved Fernando being dropped behind enemy lines and he was under 21 years old. Naturally Anna refused.

Ugo off to war, posing with his sister Bice c.1943

Ironically, when Ugo joined up, his regiment was drafted to Italy not far from Valvori. The Italians had capitulated by then, but as a British-Italian serving in the British army, he was taking a risk. Not to be outdone by her brothers, Lina joined the Auxiliary Territorial Services (ATS), leaving Bice and Alda to run the shops. Like many women who joined the ATS, Lina was first employed as a cook. As the war progressed she found herself among three hundred ATS personnel who were trained to operate searchlights and Kinetheodolite cameras. These had the ability to track an enemy plane's flight and trajectory data accurately.

Lina Rossi in her ATS uniform

In February 1941, a string of bombs fell on Southend damaging Southend Central railway station and the London Hotel which was on the corner of Southend High Street and Tyler's Avenue. Several people who had been at a dance there were brought into Rossi's Milk Bar at 99 High Street for medical treatment. Doctors treated the most serious cases on the tables in the shop. The shop stayed open all day and all night, keeping the helpers supplied with food and drink.

Pietro Rossi had been interned on the Isle of Wight and his wife Luisa stayed in Italy for the duration of the war with their youngest children Antonio and Iolanda. Pietro and Luisa had had to close their premises due to the seafront being used for military purposes. They weren't alone. Between 1939 and 1942, Southend became part of the restricted coastal zone. Road signs and the name of stations were removed and there were check points on the A127 and the A13, where police would stop pedestrians and traffic and inspect everyone's identity cards. People had to carry their identity cards at all times or face severe penalties. There were police carrying out checks at all the railway stations inside the zone and anyone who wasn't resident in the town could be turned back. Southend became virtually inaccessible to non-residents who didn't have an official reason to enter the town. The seafront itself became desolate, with anti-tank blocks and coils of barbed wire preventing access to the beach. The open-air swimming pool on Westcliff promenade was drained, the Kursaal fairground was boarded up and the pier was commandeered by the Royal Navy, so that troop ships could embark and land there.

According to family members who lived through those years, the town was full of soldiers and sailors, rather than day-trippers, and businesses like Pietro's on the seafront had no choice but to close for the duration of the war. They were unable to trade again until 1946.

Agostino was more fortunate and his shops in Southend High Street remained open throughout the war years, run by Bice, Lina and Alda between 1940 and 1943, while he and Anna were away in Hounslow. It was difficult to get enough sugar, milk and milk powder because of rationing. After the travel restrictions were lifted in 1942, a man came into one of the shops and offered the girls some milk powder on the black market; they accepted the offer without consulting Agostino, with disastrous results. Fernando, who happened to be home on leave from the army for a few days, was asked to drive up to London and pick up the milk powder. He had to meet someone who would be waiting for him in a blue van on a bridge next to Yardley's fragrance and soap factory in Stratford. He set off with his younger brother Ugo and they arrived after dark at the appointed time and place. They tasted the milk powder before handing over any money. It seemed fine, but when they got home and opened the containers, they discovered that just the top layer was milk powder; the rest was powdered chalk!

Without ice cream the business was struggling. They were only able to sell tea, coffee and toast. The town was full of soldiers, who would come into the shop hungry and ask for hot food, among them Lina's future husband Harry Price, who was posted to the barracks in Shoeburyness before his regiment was sent to East Africa. Agostino and Anna felt sorry for the men, and the family decided to start cooking chips, beans and soya links, which were sausages made from soya and bread. From then on, the shop was never empty. They were kept busy for fourteen hours a day, seven days a week. It was hard work.

After the war, the family continued to run the two shops in the High Street, plus the Argyll Café, which was attached to the Argyll Hotel on the corner of Prittlewell Square and Westcliff Parade, opposite the famous bandstand. Fernando was still keen to go back to Italy and study for a degree at a university in Rome, but Agostino said that he was needed to work in the shops with the rest of the family. He ran the shop at 37-39 High Street with his sister Alda, her husband Bill Wells and Aurelio. Fred ran the Milk Bar with his wife Pina and his sisters, Bice (who married Gianni Volante in 1948) and Lina, while Ugo and his wife Irma ran the Argyll Café.

In 1950, Agostino was diagnosed with cancer. Following an operation, he travelled to Valvori to recuperate, where he died on 6th December 1950. He left a widow, three sons, three daughters and several grandchildren.

Milk bar founder

Mr M. A. Rossi

MR. MASSIMILIANO AGOS-TINO ROSSI, one of Southend's leading traders and founder of Rossi's milk bars, died on Wednesday.

He had gone to his home town of Valori near Cassino in Southern Italy, to recuperate from an operation. When it was known that he was seriously ill, two of his sons flew from England to be at his bedside.

Sixty-one-year-old Mr. Rossi first came to England when he was 13. He started in business at the beginning of the 1930's, and soon his name became synonymous with the best in local light refreshment and catering.

Trade flourished a n d h e owned three of the leading milk-bars in the town.

MR ROSSI

The funeral took place at Valori on Thursday.

He leaves a widow and two sons.

Obituary for Agostino reported 6th January 1950. The report is inaccurate as he left a widow, 3 sons and 3 daughters.

Chapter 6

Making and Selling Ice Cream

Fernando making the ice cream 1961

When Agostino first started making ice cream he would have used a thick cream that Italians called 'fior di latte' and a sugar syrup mixed together in a 'sorbetierre' which was a metal container, made of pewter in the early days of ice cream making. The sorbetierre fitted inside a wooden bucket and chunks of ice and brine were packed around it to bring the temperature below freezing. The mixture for making ice cream had to be stirred by hand until it froze; it was really hard work. Ice had to be bought by traders - butchers, grocers, caterers and ice cream manufacturers - who needed to 'refrigerate' or freeze their produce. Agostino may have bought ice from G. Martinalli who had his premises in Guilford Road, Southend.

By the late 1940s refrigeration was becoming common place, and there were freezing machines to churn the ice cream, which ran on electricity and gas. This meant that larger quantities of ice cream could be made. The milk was boiled in huge stainless-steel vats and once it was heated Agostino would add milk powder, sugar, butter, cornflower, vanilla pods and alginate to the milk. Alginate was made from seaweed and was used to make the ice cream more viscous. I remember the wonderful smell the vanilla pods gave off as the milk was heated when Fernando was making the ice cream many years later, using the same natural ingredients his father had used. The mixture or 'mix' as it was called by the family was boiled then pasteurised for twenty minutes. Once pasteurised, it had to be cooled quickly and was trickled over a cold tubular frame which reduced the temperature. It was then transferred to stainless steel milk churns each of which held 10 gallons, and it was then stored in walk-in fridges at the back of the shop.

When it was needed, the mix was taken to the rooms below the shops where motors ran compressor freezers, capable of freezing large quantities of ice cream at a time. The freezers were deep, cylindrical, stainless steel drums, which had vertical blades fitted tightly to the sides. The drums rotated and when they were at freezing point, the ice cream mix was poured into them. It gradually froze as it came into contact with the drum, while the blades scraped it away from the sides. The ice cream had to be taken from the freezer at just the right moment, with a large scoop. If it was frozen for too long, it would become too solid to scoop out and would spoil. It was transferred into stainless steel tubs ready to sell in the shop. In both shops, the filled tubs were put on to a dumb waiter type lift and sent up through a trap door in the floor behind the counter of the shop above. From there it could be lifted onto the ice cream stall. When you were running out of ice cream you rang a bell under the counter and a fresh tub would shoot up through a trap door in the floor. It always made me jump, even when I was expecting it!

All equipment had to be thoroughly cleaned and sterilized and the floors scrubbed each day. I remember Fernando, his brother-in-law Bill Wells and his uncle Aurelio clad in white overalls, wellington boots and yellow oil cloth aprons, scouring and sterilising everything with a special green coloured liquid, before each new batch was made; and again afterwards. There were regular checks from the health inspector who would take samples away to make sure the ice cream was always of the highest standard; and it always was. Ice cream or fresh ice cream mix had to be delivered daily to various outlets as well as all the Rossi shops, and in the summer months it was hard work keeping up with the demand.

Fernando with staff at Rossi's 37-39 High St in the late 1950s

Fernando, Patsy Brady the manageress and Nina Salvatore, a family friend

All the staff had to learn how to make the famous Rossi cornet. The ice cream had to be exactly the right texture so that when you loaded it onto the large flat spoon and scraped it onto one side of the cone, it would stay there. Then you had to stretch it and flick your wrist in such a way that the ice cream formed a loop which you had to attach to the other side of the cone. There was a definite knack to it, and if the ice cream was too soft or too hard it wouldn't work. It took a bit of practice but when we were learning, we were allowed to eat some of the mistakes we made. We were deliberately slow to learn. Delicious! The ice cream stalls would have stacks of cones on one side of the counter. They were a great temptation to some of the young rascals of the day, who would ask:

"'Ave yer got any broken cornets, miss?" If you answered "No!" they would grab at the cones and crush a couple shouting "Well yer 'ave now!" and they would run off laughing their heads off.

As well as cornets, wafers and tubs, customers could buy '99' cornets with the added treat of a Cadbury flake stuck in it. Ice cream also formed the base of frothy milkshakes. It was used to make iced coffee and added to glasses of *Pepsi Cola* or *7 Up* lemonade, making the drinks fizz and froth as soon as the scoop of ice cream was added. Customers also ordered mouth-watering Knickerbocker Glories, Banana Splits with chocolate sauce and Peach Melbas with layers of ice cream, peaches, and raspberry sauce.

Anna Rossi serving ice cream

During the 1950s and 1960s, day-trippers continued to flock into Southend, especially at the weekend, and would stop for a 'Rossi' on their way to the seafront. There were often long queues requiring two people to serve, one to make the cornets and the other to take the money. Gallons of ice cream were sold in a day. Less trade was done in the winter months, but throughout the year, shoppers would come into Rossi's for a cup of tea or coffee and buy sandwiches and cakes as well. They also bought cooked meals like sausage and chips, hot dogs and delicious homemade steak burgers which were actually made with real steak, minced and seasoned in the shop. These were very popular garnished with a layer of fried onions and French mustard. People working in the High Street came into Rossi's for lunch and the shops were also popular meeting places for couples in the evenings. Every night rows of mugs, coffee cups and tea cups had to be laid out ready for the rush as soon as the cinemas turned out. People would fill the shops and buy a hot drink before catching the last bus home.

Early on Sunday mornings, all the shelves behind the counters had to be emptied of crockery and thoroughly washed. There were no dishwashers so on Sundays, all the cups were given an extra clean with a brush and scouring powder. In the summer months, this had to be done before the waves of day-trippers flooded from the stations. You could always tell when a train had just pulled into Southend Central railway station. The shops would suddenly fill up, and the queue for ice cream would start to grow.

In the early 1960s there was great excitement when a brand new Carpigiani machine was installed in the shop. The Carpigiani was one of the first of its kind in the town, which could serve two flavours of ice cream at once. It was a great novelty. Customers could have a cornet with strawberry and vanilla which came out like striped toothpaste, as well as vanilla, coffee and even pistachio on its own. Most people still preferred the original ice cream though; served with a spoon. It was impossible to make a wafer with ice cream from the machine; it wasn't firm enough because the consistency was slightly different. The same mix was poured into the machine, but beaters added air to it. It was kept frozen at a temperature which allowed it to be extracted through the nozzles. The advantage was that it used less mix as the air bulked it out. It also stayed frozen in the machine, whereas the ice cream served the traditional way from the steel tubs with a spoon, tended to melt on top and round the edges, especially in hot weather. This was minimal on a busy day, but if trade was slack the melted ice cream couldn't be used.

As café owners and ice cream sellers in the town installed their own Carpigiani machines, Fernando, Fred and Bill were kept busy supplying them with different flavoured mixes. They also supplied ice cream for weddings and various events in the town. The family was always very generous and regularly donated ice cream to church fêtes, and many charitable organisations. They were members of the Ice Cream Alliance and often won awards for their ice cream.

Fernando showing the author Patricia how to use the new
Carpigiani machine in April 1961

Chapter 7

Memories

Author Patricia with Fernando in 1969

Extra members of staff were always taken on by the Rossi ice cream venues for the summer; mostly students like me. The radio was usually on in the shop. We loved the charts show '*Pick of the Pops*' and I remember songs like '*Anyone who had a heart*' and '*Go now*'. We listened to Elvis Presley, Cliff Richard and later the Beatles. Their songs would have us singing along between customers.

On Saturdays when the evening shift came on at 6.30pm, there would be a fight to get to the mirrors in the cloak room, to put on another layer of black eyeliner and mascara and back comb our hair. We would slip into our winkle picker shoes, and maybe put on a new dress or blouse that we had purchased in our lunch break from local boutiques such as Martin Ford's in the High Street or Renee's in York Road arcade; buying all we could afford. We would then head for one of the cinemas in the town, either the Ritz, the Rivoli, or the Odeon, to watch the latest film and we always sat in the front row on the left-hand side of the circle. There were so many wonderful films to choose from. We fell in love with Omar Sharif in *Lawrence of Arabia*, Tony Curtis in *Spartacus* and Steve McQueen in *The Great Escape*. We didn't sleep properly for weeks after seeing Alfred Hitchcock's *Psycho*, but my favourite film of the sixties was *The Graduate* with Dustin Hoffman and Anne Bancroft. Sometimes we would go to the bowling alley on the pier instead, and we often went back to Rossi's afterwards, sitting on the other side of the counter as customers for a change and sipping our drinks before heading home.

It wasn't unusual for policemen or local tradesmen to pop into the kitchen at the back of the shops for a quick cup of tea and a snack. I used to love the banter when the likes of Johnny Marwood, a local journalist, or Ken Woolcott, the photographer who had his office above the shop, came in for a cup of tea. Meanwhile the local 'down and outs', as they were referred to then, knew exactly where in the shop to stand in order to catch Fernando's eye and he would always give them something to eat and a couple of pound notes to put in their pockets.

Members of staff were very well looked after. We could have more or less what we liked to eat at break time and lunch time, up to a certain value, so that people didn't take advantage. I was brought up just after the war, when food was still on ration, so when I first started working at the shop in 1959, to me butter was still a luxury; we always had margarine at home. The Rossis used real butter in their sandwiches, rolls and buns; and the buttered Bath buns they sold with sugar crystals on top were my idea of heaven.

I was particularly lucky because sometimes on a Saturday afternoon, if Alda, Lina and Bice were all working in the shops, I would be asked to take their children to a matinee at the cinema. Alda would give me a bag full of chocolate biscuits, and money to pay for tickets and sweets. I would get to see the latest Disney film, and when we got back, Alda invariably told me to keep the change. What a treat, and I still got my wages!

Anna and Agostino's grand children went to Sacred Heart School, St Helen's School or Lindisfarne Prep. School in Westcliff on Sea. In the 1960s when they were small, some of the grandchildren were collected from school at midday and taken to have lunch with their Nonna Anna, in the family room above the shop at 37-39 High Street. One of Alda's daughters, Karen, remembers that all the children used to come into the shop through the milk house at the back, where the ice cream was made. It used to scare the living daylights out of her. After lunch, the children had to go through it again to get to the door which opened into Clarence Street, where Karen's father or one of her uncles, would be waiting with the van to take them all back to school. The noisy clunking of the machinery as it churned the milk and filled the place with steam really frightened Karen, and she would stand at one end working up the courage to negotiate the passageway between the machines; then dash through with her hands over her ears. She says that noisy machinery has frightened her ever since.

Karen also remembers that occasionally she and her sisters, brother and cousins were permitted to go down stairs into the shop to get an ice cream. Karen says: "We were never allowed behind the bar while the shop was open, and we stood obediently on a line marking the beginning of the 'out of bounds' area. If our toes went over, the manageress Patsy Brady would make us move back. She would ask if we had eaten our dinner, and if not, there would be no treat. We had to go through the same ritual every time! The one Rossi delight we were never, ever allowed was a Knickerbocker

Glory; a tall dessert glass full of tinned peaches, pears and ice cream drenched in thick, sugary, raspberry syrup and topped with a cherry, chocolate flake and two wafers. To me it was the most beautiful, mouth-watering creation I had ever seen, and I would stare longingly as I watched them being prepared for customers. Sadly, it was considered far too much of an extravagance for us small children and I never got to taste the delights of this iconic dessert."

Anna and Agostino's grandson Chris Price also has fond memories of being at the shop after school. Chris says: "Most of my memories are about the shop at 99 High Street where my mother Lina, my uncle Fred and Aunty Bice worked. I would arrive at the shop after school, have some tea and watch Uncle Fred freezing the ice cream, while Zia Aldina made the steak burgers for the shop, using a press where she put minced steak between two sheets of circular greaseproof paper. Occasionally I would walk to the other shop at 37-39 High Street and visit my Nonna (grandma) who would offer me more tea and ice cream. I would make a beeline for uncle Fernando who would tell me jokes and show me how to make the ice cream."

Fred's sons Dino and Roberto remember their childhood in the shop too. Dino says: "I remember drinking fresh coffee early on Christmas morning after Mass at St Helen's Church; I was about six at the time. We had one of the first Gaggia coffee machines in Southend which used freshly ground coffee and it was awesome. At times the Milk Bar was a second home; I ate there, played there and sometimes helped out with washing up, even though I had to stand on a milk crate to reach the sink. I suppose the shop was my crèche as both parents worked there but this was normal for me. The basement was always busy, as much of the food preparation was done there, it was where the staff had their breaks and the local street 'bobby' could often be found having his break and a cup of tea. My dad Fred froze the ice cream there each day for the shop, and I can still remember the taste. Best ice cream ever! As I got older, I was allowed to wander further afield and roam the High Street visiting such places as Woolworths, Owen Wallis, Pier Hill or the Talza (Victoria) Arcade. The High Street seemed a much nicer place in those days." Sadly, Dino died on Sunday 29th October 2017. His brother Roberto also remembered the constant warnings from his father not to go near the ice cream while it churned because of the sharp blades, but he loved watching it swirling around and would stand on his tip-toes peering into the drum.

In 1960, Anna and Agostino's son Ugo and his wife Irma decided to branch out on their own. They took over a shop in Alexander Street and converted it into a very smart coffee bar and restaurant called 'La Tana' (The Den) where they sold wonderful homemade pasta dishes. It was the beginning of a love affair with Italian food for many people in the town – especially me!

Left to Right: Pina (Fred's wife), Irma (Ugo's wife), Ugo, Fernando and Fred

Chapter 8

Changing Times

Rossi's kiosk in the High Street which was opened in 1969.
Credit Philip Rosz

At some point during the 1960s, the family decided that the shop at 37-39 High Street needed up-dating and it was time to extend the lease. They were shocked to discover that in spite of an agreement Agostino had made many years earlier with the freeholders of the property, the freeholders now wanted to sell the premises to developers and refused to renew the lease. This was a very difficult moment for Agostino and Anna's family. The Milk Bar at 99 High Street was doing very well, but there wasn't enough room beneath that shop to install the whole set up needed to make the ice cream mix as well as freeze it. Without 37-39 High Street it wasn't practical to continue trading.

Added to this, local people's shopping habits were changing. By 1967, the pedestrianisation at the top end of the High Street had begun, meaning passing trade at the lower end was slowing down. The crowds of customers, who used to come into the shops when the cinemas turned out, had diminished with the arrival of colour television. People weren't going to the cinema as often as they used to. Package holidays abroad had become affordable and popular, many flying out from Southend Airport, and there was a noticeable decline in the number of day trippers in the summer months. So, in 1969 both shops were closed, and the Milk Bar was sold.

Fernando wasn't too sorry to see the shops close. Since the death of Agostino, he had shouldered most of the responsibility for running the business and had begun to find it all very stressful. It was fortunate that I had chosen teaching as a career. By the time all three of our children were at school, Fernando had health problems, and in 1979 he was advised to give up work. I had been teaching French part-time at a local secondary school, but in 1980 I was offered a full-time post at Our Lady of Lourdes Primary School in Leigh, where our children were at school. I took it and worked there until retirement in 2005.

Fred and Ugo went on to run cafés of their own for a few years; Fred's in Westcliff and Ugo's in Shoeburyness. Meanwhile, Pietro and Luisa's branch of the Rossi's Ice Cream business, by now run by their son Antonio (Tony) and daughters Maria and Iolanda, was less affected by the changes because their shop was located along the seafront. However, realising that they were going to have to make all their own ice cream mix from scratch, they had a factory built in Lucy Road in 1967. Their business continued to thrive, winning many prestigious awards.

Marine Parade in the 1970s. Credit Philip Rosz

Rossi's shop in Marine Parade in the 1970s. Credit Philip Rosz

The trade at the Marine Parade and Western Esplanade shops had always been seasonal, but the factory at Lucy Road enabled them to supply a whole fleet of ice cream vans and sell ice cream in litre containers which could be purchased at any time of the year. They produced ice lollies in many flavours, delicious lemon sorbet, blocks of ice cream and a variety of alternatives to cornets, wafers and tubs, like 'Screwballs' which were in a plastic cone and had a ball of chewing gum at the bottom. The 'Oyster' shell was popular. It contained marshmallow and could be filled with a large spoonful of ice cream. A particular favourite of mine was the 'Cassata' they made at Christmas time which was vanilla ice cream mixed with candied fruit and shaped like a Christmas pudding.

In 1969, Tony and his sisters acquired a kiosk at the top of the High Street which was always very busy in the summer months. They were frequently asked if they were the 'real' Rossi's once the High Street shops had closed, so a crown and the word 'Original' was added to their logo. The traditional method of serving ice cream from a tub still remained popular, and in 1983, Maria Rossi was invited onto the TV show '*The Generation Game*' to demonstrate this method of serving ice cream. Sadly, Maria, Tony and Iolanda had no family to carry on the business. Iolanda kept the business going after first Maria and then Tony died; but after Iolanda's death in 2007, her husband Regalo Di Mascio decided to sell the factory in Lucy Road, their Westcliff kiosk and the lease on their premises on Marine Parade.

Today, the Rossi ice cream business continues under new ownership. It is no longer a family run business, but still produces award-winning ice cream. In 2010, the company gained accreditation allowing them to supply ASDA, Morrison's and Co-op stores throughout the county and surrounding areas. Available through independent retailers, Rossi products are also supplied to many hotels including Bourne Leisure and Holiday Inn.

In addition to the original flavours, the company now creates bespoke flavours, like the vanilla ice cream with a red and blue ripple which was made for a British Airways campaign at Heathrow Airport. In 2015, an array of internationally themed flavours was produced for InsureAndGo.com as part of their 'Around the World in 80 Scoops' promotional event. The following August, inspired by an ice cream experiment in America, the company became the first known UK manufacturer to produce jet black vanilla ice cream. I can't help wondering what Agostino would have made of that.

In the final months of 2016 and almost 50 years since it was built, the Lucy Road factory closed, and the company moved into new, larger and more efficient premises situated at Temple Farm Industrial Estate in Southend. The new premises have better warehousing, production, freezing and storage facilities, enabling the company to cater for the increased demand for Rossi Ice Cream products. In company director Colin Gray's words: "Rossi Ice Cream continues to go from strength to strength and the move is down to many factors as we continue to take the business forward whilst still maintaining the Rossi heritage."

On a visit to the newly opened premises, I was impressed by the room where employees must 'gown up' and 'scrub up' before entering the area where the ice cream is made. It made me think of a surgeon entering an operating theatre. I was fascinated by a row of spotless white wellington boots worn only in the huge production area. When Agostino started making ice cream to sell on the streets of Glasgow over a century ago, he could never have imagined how his small business would one day grow into such a large and celebrated enterprise.

Most of Agostino's grandchildren and great grandchildren still live in the Southend area. They have various careers and apart from Agostino's granddaughter Sandra Donnelly and her family, none are involved in the catering business. Sandra and her son James own a successful bar called Ugo's in the Broadway, Leigh on Sea, named after her father Ugo Rossi. Sandra's younger son Joe and her daughter Lucy have opened an ice cream parlour together called 'Poco Gelato' in Elm Road, Leigh on Sea. It's definitely in the genes! I think that Agostino would be rather pleased that things have gone full circle and that Joe and Lucy make delicious ice cream based on his recipe, now using the best organic ingredients and producing many unusual and contemporary flavours as well as the traditional ones. The ice cream is made on the premises and served in the traditional way, with a scoop. They supply restaurants throughout Essex and across London and have an on-line delivery service.

Photos Emma Donnelly

Agostino, Anna and their children, Bice, Lina, Fred, Fernando, Ugo and Alda are no longer alive. I like to think of them all, together somewhere in the ether, enjoying a family meal and a glass of wine, laughing and happy, the way that we all remember them. They were an honest, hard-working and generous family and their descendants are proud of their Rossi heritage. A tattered handwritten copy of Agostino's original recipe, with instructions for making 100 gallons of ice cream still exists. It is a treasured family keepsake, kept in a safe place just in case it should ever be needed again!

Further reading, sources and acknowledgements:

National Archives

Scottish Archives: Valuation Rolls 1920 -1928

Kelly's Directory Southend-on-Sea 1927 and 1933

Ice Merchant Electoral Roll Southend-on-Sea 1937

Chelmsford Chronicle, Essex Newsman and *Glasgow Herald* Archives

BBC Radio 4 archives Tom Conti interviews internees and their families.